The Web Designer's Client Handbook *

*Everything You Always Wanted to Know About Websites But Were Afraid to Ask Your Web Designer

by Keith B. Darrell

The Web Designer's Client Handbook
By Keith B. Darrell
Amber Book Company
U.S.A.

2006

Library of Congress Card Catalog Card Number:
2006908162
The Web Designer's Client Handbook / Keith B. Darrell

ISBN: 0-9771611-1-0

First printing September 2006

 The Web Designer's Client Handbook

PREFACE

I would like to thank both my clients and my fellow web designers who have, albeit often unintentionally, contributed anecdotally to the creation of this handbook.

The Web Designer's Client Handbook fills a desperate need. It is an answer to a plethora of questions plaguing both web designers and their clients — "Can you believe what my client wants now?" • "How can I make my client understand?" • "Why can't my website look exactly the way I want it to?"

This handbook paves the way for the transition from the client's nebulous dream to the web designer's application of craft. From conceptualization to execution, the client and the web designer must be on the same wavelength. Many clients take the World Wide Web for granted and do not have a true understanding of its workings or limitations, which can result in a frustrating experience for both client and designer. *The Web Designer's Client Handbook* was written to ease that transition.

The Web Designer's Client Handbook

INTRODUCTION

Seldom has there been so great a need for a book such as *The Web Designer's Client Handbook* to be written. Most people are expert in their own businesses but are clueless when it comes to transporting that business to the Internet. The average person knows nothing of the limitations of web technology or what constitutes good design. Often they do not even consider applying common business principles, such as branding, to their online presence. They often approach the web designer with vague ideas and unreasonable expectations. Web designers, on the other hand, often do a poor job of communicating to their clients why something the client wants is either technologically not feasible or esthetically undesirable from a design standpoint.

There are certain basic concepts that clients need to understand before engaging a web designer to build their website. Either the designer must educate the client or the client must go out on his own and educate himself. Often the designer is too busy or impatient to do so and clients have not had the resources available to them to learn. Until now.

Introduction

The Web Designer's Client Handbook fills the gap between the designer and the client, providing the contextual background necessary for the client to understand both the limitations of web technology and certain elements and fundamental principles of website design. Web designers should stock up on copies of this handbook and give them out to every new or potential client. And anyone considering hiring a web designer to build her site should first read this short book from cover-to-cover!

Table of Contents

Contents

CHAPTER ONE

WHY YOU NEED A WEBSITE

"WHY SHOULD MY BUSINESS have a website?," you may well ask. After all, you may have run your business very successfully for many years without a website. You may feel that your business has nothing to do with the Internet, or perhaps you simply have no products that can be sold online. You may be concerned about the expense of setting up a website, or maybe you're just intimidated by this "new-fangled technology."

So why should you have a website? There are many reasons, but perhaps the most compelling reason to have a website for your business is that your competitors already have one! In the business world, in order to stay competitive, you have to keep up with your competitors. What's more, your customers shop around — they've seen your competitors; they *expect* your business to have a website!

Chapter One

The Internet is global. Anyone, anywhere in the world can get on the Internet and see your website. The number of individuals and businesses establishing a presence on the Internet has exploded. Wherever you look (TV, magazines, movies, or radio) you see or hear "www.companyname.com." Your customers are already looking at your competitors' websites; shouldn't they be looking at yours?

The Internet allows you to provide a multimedia experience for visitors to your business' website. Website visitors can gather information, compare products and services, communicate with your business (through e-mail or online forms) requesting help with a product or service, or read a list of frequently asked questions (FAQs) to resolve problems with a product or service purchased offline. A company website can save time and money in customer service. It's also an excellent way to advertise and market your products and services because it's like having an advertisement in all of the Yellow Pages and newspapers across the world without the huge costs.

In fact, contrary to the notion that it is very expensive to set up and maintain a business website, your website may be the most cost-effective advertising, sales, and customer relations tool you will ever have. Dollar-for-dollar, there is no way to reach so many people for so little! As a successful business person, you know the value of marketing and advertising, because you probably already have an advertisement in the phone book and have or would like to have radio and television

 The Web Designer's Client Handbook

commercials. A business website is a permanent advertisement on the Internet for people to access 24 hours a day and learn more about your business. Additionally, there is practically no limit to the number of pages that your website can have. Imagine placing your entire inventory or sales catalogue on your website for less than the cost of a single display ad! And no more waiting for the next issue to update an ad; changes can be made to your website immediately! Customers will also appreciate the convenience of resolving problems by e-mail as opposed to waiting for hours "on hold" for telephone customer support.

A business website can be one of three types, depending on its purpose:

- *Informational* (to create awareness of the business),
- *Product-oriented* (to provide specific details of products and services), and
- *E-commerce* (to facilitate purchase transactions online).

For example, suppose you have a service-oriented business, such as a tax preparation firm. Since you have no products to sell, you would require an informational website to advertise your services, showcase your experience, provide directions and a map to your office, and list your office hours. You could add comments from satisfied customers and pictures of your office. You might even include a tax tips newsletter to keep visitors returning to your website.

However, suppose you have developed a do-it-yourself tax preparation software program that you wish to market. Now you will need a product-oriented website, since the focus of your website has changed from creating awareness of your business in the minds of the public to providing specific detail about your product. The website may then provide a list of wholesale or retail outlets where your product can be obtained, or instruct customers to print out your order form and mail a check to you, or call in an order by phone.

You may discover that many customers prefer the convenience of placing orders directly online. In this case, you will need to convert to an e-commerce website. There are two payment methods available to e-commerce websites; online payment and offline payment. Online payment requires a payment gateway, such as a merchant bank or PayPal, to enable merchants to authorize, settle, and manage credit card or electronic check transactions. Alternatively, your website can have a form that collects and forwards the credit card information to you, which you would then manually process offline.

Next you must decide if your e-commerce website will be *static* or *dynamic*. A static website remains the same every time the viewer sees it unless the page is modified by the designer. A dynamic website is one whose content is regenerated every time a viewer visits or reloads the website. If you have a dozen items, a static page consisting of a table with 12 cells each with a picture and text description of each item and a "Buy Now" button may suffice. However, if you have hundreds of items it might be preferable to use a dynamic solution such as a shopping cart. One advantage of such a dynamic solution is that it allows viewers to search the database for specific terms and then regenerates a page containing only the items that the viewer was searching for. (A disadvantage to dynamic pages is that while content in your website's database is searchable on within your website it would not be searchable by external search engines like Yahoo or Google).

Chapter Two

 The Web Designer's Client Handbook

CHAPTER TWO

PROFESSIONAL VS. AMATEUR DESIGN

O.K., YOU'RE CONVINCED that your business needs a website. But instead of viewing it as an opportunity for increasing profits, you are cringing at the thought of yet another expense! You can hear the gears churning away in your mind as you try to figure out a way to minimize the cost of your new website. Didn't the kid who mows your lawn mention that he had built a website? Or what about that website-building software you saw at the computer store? Wouldn't that be cheaper than hiring a professional web designer?

Of course it would be cheaper! Then again, you may recall the old saying, "pennywise and pound foolish." Your website's design and appearance is critical. For many potential customers your website is their first, and possibly only, impression of your business. Remember the old adage "You never get a second chance to make a first impression!" Your potential customers may make judgments about you, your professionalism, your expertise, or your business solely based on their impression of your website. A disorganized, poorly laid-out website may convey the impression that your business is equally disorganized. Pages with misspelled words and poor grammar may lead visitors to infer ignorance, incompetence, or merely sloppiness on your part—not traits you want associated with your business. And if your pages do not load properly because of poor design (which is very common with inexperienced designers) or your links do not work (the dreaded "404 – Page Not Found" error message) then your inexperienced designer's incompetence may be transferred to you and your business in the minds of your website visitors. Your website should instill visitors with confidence in your competence, not do the opposite! Your customers will not appreciate your frugalness in saving a few pennies; in fact, a cheaply-designed website may lead them to believe that you will also cut corners in the work you do for them as well.

Still not convinced? Let's examine the choices. Sure, you can buy a web page kit off the shelf from the computer store. It may cost anywhere from $80 to $200. And then you first have to spend hours learning how to use the software before you can even begin your page. But that's not the real problem. All pre-packaged web design software has one major flaw—the software is limited. It's cookie-cutter stuff. It will give you only so many options and that's it. You get a stripped-down basic web page template that looks like the page everyone else made with that software. Do you really want to look like everyone else? There are billions of people, worldwide, on the Internet. You need to stand out, especially if you have a business you are trying to promote. Creativity — it doesn't come in a box!

Choice two, hire the high school kid advertising his "web page design" business with neighborhood flyers and on the Internet. He'll work cheap! He already owns a web page kit and wants to use it to make your page. He needs the practice. Experience — it doesn't come in a box!

Choice three is the "template designer." You can usually recognize them by their pricing structure, *e.g.,* "4 pages for $500." These people are usually self-taught (they bought a few HTML (Hyper Text Mark-up Language) books and read some articles online) and rely on software-produced templates. However, it takes more than a passing knowledge of HTML (the language used by computers to format web pages for your browser) and Microsoft Front Page software to design a good website. A web designer must also have a sense of design, layout, usability, and site navigation. Self-taught "web designers" usually only have a limited skill set — they have studied the areas that were of interest to them but not the whole "Internet picture." Often they only work with one browser and are surprised to learn that their finished websites may look significantly different when viewed in other browsers (as discussed in Chapter Four). And templates are easily spotted. Your final product should be as unique as you are!

If you are a serious business person, you have only one real choice — a professional web designer. The hallmarks of a professional web designer are training, certification, a varied skill set, and a commitment to continuing education to stay current on the latest trends in this fast-evolving industry.

There are many schools that offer web design programs — not merely a single course but entire curricula devoted to the various aspects of creating and maintaining websites. Your web designer's background should include training from such a program — not merely a course at the local adult education class. Certification by a professional web design organization is evidence that your designer has met the requirement of completing multiple classes on various areas of web design and passed rigorous examinations to prove his or her knowledge and competence. The Certified Internet Webmaster (CIW) program is the world's largest and fastest-growing Internet certification program. The CIW certification program is explained in detail on their website, www.ciwcertified.com.

The web designer you choose should also have (or have access to) the necessary skill set to do the job required. He may not possess all the skills himself, but he should have associates or affiliates who complement his own skill set. It is not possible for your designer to be expert with every software program and every programming language or new technology that may be required to implement your website, but as long as he works with others who have whatever expertise may be required within their skill sets, he or she can do a professional job on your website. Think of your designer as a general contractor building your house. At some point he may have to call in, in essence, several sub-contractors. But instead of plumbers, roofers, and electricians he may bring in PERL or Java programmers, Flash Action Script or JavaScript scripters, graphic designers, Flash designers, or search engine optimizers. In fact, bringing in additional expertise when a project becomes complex is a sign of a good web designer.

The amazing thing about the World Wide Web is that the technology is constantly changing. HTML has been revised many times, as have web standards. New versions of web design software are released continually and the web designer must familiarize himself with the changes made in each revision. Web browsers are also continually redesigned and the web designer must stay aware of how changes in browsers will affect the appearance of existing websites, and also how to optimize both future and existing pages for these new browsers. New technologies are introduced almost daily. Some, such as Macromedia Flash, will become new standards in web design, while others will merely be flash-in-the pans. As a professional, your web designer stays current on the latest trends to assure that your website keeps up with the latest advances in web technology.

Chapter Two

Cheaper is not better. Learn to look past the bottom line on a design proposal. Your website is YOU on the Internet. It is the image that you project to the world. How your potential customers perceive you and your business will ultimately rest in the hands of the person you choose to design your website. Choose well.

CHAPTER THREE

GETTING STARTED

Designating Your Authorized Contact Person

You've heard the clichés — "a ship has only one captain;" "too many cooks spoil the brew." Your website project should have only one contact person — specifically designated and authorized by you — to serve as the liaison between your company and your web designer. Allowing multiple members of your organization to transmit conflicting instructions to your designer is a recipe for chaos and will likely delay your project and increase its costs. Choose one person to be in charge of dealing with your web designer and try to communicate all instructions in writing, preferably by e-mail. Sending all corrections, changes, and additions to the website by e-mail to your designer will limit problems caused by miscommunication and serve to create a paper trail if needed.

Chapter Three

Choosing Your Domain Name

Your website is like a piece of real estate on the World Wide Web. And like any parcel of real estate, your website has a unique address, called an IP (Internet Protocol) address. IP addresses consist of four groups of three-digit numbers, each group separated by a period, and range from 0.0.0.0 to 255.255.255.255. Since dotted decimal numeric IP addresses are hard to remember, the Domain Name System was set up to associate the numeric IP address with a familiar name, such as www.mycompany.com. When you type a domain name into your browser it queries a name server (a machine on the Internet that obtains the numeric IP address and then uses that address to direct its requests to the right computer on the Internet). The web page then displays in your browser.

To obtain a domain name for your website, either you or your web designer must contact a domain name registrar. A quick search of the registrar's database will reveal if the desired name is available or if someone has beaten you to it. Once a domain name is registered, it can take up to three working days before it can be used and is visible on the Internet.

Defining Your Website

Now it's time to make some decisions. What will be the purpose of your website? As we discussed in Chapter One, you must decide if your website will be an informational, product-oriented, or e-commerce website. What is the nature of your business? Is it service-oriented? Is it a new business about to be launched? In those cases, an informational website to create awareness of your business may be all that is required. But if you have a product to sell, then a product-oriented website would be the right choice. And if you choose to sell that product online, an e-commerce website becomes necessary. Knowing the purpose of your website allows your web designer to determine how many and what type of pages the site will require. Some basic pages might include Home Page, About Us, FAQ (Frequently Asked Questions), Contact Us, Site Map, Terms of Use, Privacy Policy, Forms, Order Terms, Payment & Shipping Info, Product Pages (if static), Shopping Cart (if dynamic), and Directions/Map. Your designer may choose not to include all of these pages or he may add pages that are relevant to your business needs.

Your designer may provide you with a worksheet where you can outline what you would like on your site. You can provide your designer with existing brochures or pamphlets that you have to help in the design process. Of course, your designer will work closely with you to suggest web page layout in accordance with HTML constraints. Often it is a good idea to diagram a flow chart of how you would like the pages to link to each other. In doing so, remember the "Three Click Rule" — no page should be more than three mouse clicks away from the home page. Viewers should not need to click more than three times to get to the desired information on your website.

Chapter Three

If you have chosen to proceed with an e-commerce site, then your next decision will be whether to have static or dynamic pages. A static website stays the same each time it is viewed unless the page is modified by the designer. A dynamic website's content regenerates whenever the page is visited or reloaded. If you have a dozen items, a static page consisting of a table with 12 cells, each with a picture and text description of each item and a "Buy Now" button may suffice. However, a dynamic solution such as a shopping cart might be preferable if you have hundreds of items. While a dynamic solution has the advantage of enabling viewers to search the database for specific terms and then regenerating a page containing only the items that the viewer was searching for, it suffers from the disadvantage that while content in your website's database is searchable on within your website it would not be searchable by external search engines like Yahoo or Google.

Website Usability

Your next consideration to plan with your designer is the style or overall look and feel of the website. Your style comes from the elements consistently carried over throughout your site. Such elements include layout, color, fonts, images, and multi-media. It is important to select a consistent color scheme throughout the site to help tie the individual pages together. Style can also be expressed through use of a metaphor to set the overall look and feel of the site. For example, one doctor's website used the metaphor of a doctor's clipboard to frame all of the pages on the site.

 The Web Designer's Client Handbook

Getting Started

A common misconception is that a "good" site must dazzle the viewer with multi-media bells and whistles; however, the reality is that the most important aspect of web design is content. People return because the website is constantly updated with new and relevant information, not to see flashy graphics. Trust your web designer's judgment on how far to go with "special effects." Remember the web adage "If it blinks, it stinks!"

Website usability may be defined as knowing how to give your viewers what they want. This further breaks down into four criteria: quality content, ease of navigation, an organized structure, and search capability. Visitors to your site should be able to find what they want easily and intuitively. Surveys have found that the most important factors to website visitors are, in order of importance: ease of use/navigation, fast download time, regularly updated information, quality of content, and organization of content. The same surveys reveal what visitors to your website do not want to see: slow loading sites, help buttons that do not help, requests for personal details before being allowed to progress into the site, irrelevant search results or no search capability, poorly organized content or having to scroll down through lots of pages to get to the information, ads (including banner ads) and pop-up windows, cluttered design, contact information that is difficult to find, compulsory music or video, cover pages, inconsistent styles, and pages that are difficult to read because of lack of contrast, changes of background, long text lines, flashing or moving elements, and pop-ups.

Hosting

Now we turn to hosting. The data that make up your website must be stored on a server, to be accessed by all of the computers that link to the Internet. Storage on such a server is called web hosting. You may be tempted to host on a "free" server. "Free" hosting is really ad-supported hosting, so you would not want to place a business website on a "free" server that will place pop-up ads and banner ads on your page. Not only would that be unprofessional, but you would have no control over the content of the ads appearing on your website! There are many firms that specialize in web hosting and your web designer may offer hosting services as well. Once again, price should not be the major factor in selecting a web host, as most firms offer hosting services within a similar price range. The more important factors are reliability and support. How reliable is the web host? While all servers go offline at some point, if only for planned maintenance or occasional problems, you do not want a host with chronic downtime. Likewise, when problems do occur (and they will) you want a host with 24-hour support that works immediately to solve the problem. Is the host knowledgeable? Are the servers large and fast? Is there 24-hour support? Is there phone support? Will the server support CGI, ASP, or any special needs? Are there charges for exceeding bandwidth, and if so, how much? What is the "uptime/downtime" ratio? Cheap hosting is not a bargain if your website is constantly offline!

You also want to make sure that your hosting company can accommodate both your present needs and future growth. Some hosts cannot support certain programming features that your site may need to run. Changing to a new host may mean, for example, that your cgi-based shopping cart will no longer function. Always check with your web designer to see if the web host will be compatible with your website needs. Also, the features offered by the hosting company may suit your present needs, but do they provide for future growth? What if your site eventually requires more space, more bandwidth, more mailboxes, more mailing lists, or more databases? Can the hosting company meet your future needs and if so at what cost?

Working With Your Designer

Remember the story of Goldilocks and the three bears? If your web designer is Goldilocks, then which bear are you? Papa Bear tells Goldilocks that he wants a "fantastic" website. It must be very stylish. He wants it to "wow" him. It should be two, no, three times better than his competitor's site. Mama Bear shows Goldilocks three loose leaf notebooks filled with ideas for the "Porridge Unlimited" website. She has designed her own fonts and has a precise "set-in-stone" sketch of how the site must look. Finally, Baby Bear arrives, having filled out the web designer's questionnaire and flow chart. Baby Bear's porridge website is "just right."

In our Goldilocks scenario, Papa Bear never really defined what he wanted. His descriptions were vague and non-specific. He just knows that he wants a "great" website but that is not much help to the designer, who is not a mind reader. Meanwhile, Mama Bear is too specific and inflexible, not allowing for variances between the print media that she is familiar with and the web. But Baby Bear, by filling out the designer's questionnaire and flow chart, has given the designer some concrete guidelines and a sense of direction while still remaining flexible enough to allow the designer to adapt his ideas to the web.

So before your initial meeting with your designer stop and think which bear you are and what you need to do to be the right bear!

Communication between you and your designer is extremely important. You need to share your vision of your finished website with your designer yet also listen to your designer's explanation of the limitations of the online medium. While you may be very familiar with the print medium from past marketing endeavors, there are many differences between the print medium and the web. In print, everyone sees the same colors, type fonts and sizes, but online colors may vary by monitor while font types and sizes may vary by operating system or user-selected preferences. In fact, on the web some viewers may choose not to view graphics or to apply their own style sheets, thereby changing the color, size, and font of your type. Readers can immediately tell how long an article or book is, but it is not immediately apparent how many pages a website may have. While readers usually start at the beginning of a book and read in a linear fashion to the end, your website visitors may follow a link or search engine to land haphazardly on a random page within your site. That is one reason why site navigation and site usability are so vital. Finally, the print medium is static whereas the web is dynamic and always changing. Your designer may complete your website project but your website will never truly be finished! By its very nature, it will always be a work-in-progress!

You want your website up as soon as possible, so you and your designer will set a deadline for your site to "go live." While most clients respond that their preferred deadline is "yesterday," the three factors that determine your deadline are the complexity of your site, the start date when your designer can fit the project into his schedule, and your readiness and cooperation in supplying text and graphic content to your designer. Obviously, if you delay supplying your designer with the content he needs to integrate into your website then your deadline may not be met. Don't procrastinate and then dump all the text and photos on your designer a week before the deadline. Likewise, many clients are very excited when they commission their website project, but as other aspects of their business demand attention the website project is often relegated to the back burner on the client's priority list. Remember, your designer has allocated a block of his schedule to working on your project; if you procrastinate and then later decide your website is a high priority item your designer at that point may be committed to other projects and you may be sent to the end of the queue!

Don't make your designer's job any harder than it already is! Submit your final drafts. Designers do not appreciate having to revise text after they have finished laying out the page.

Most custom design projects come with an estimated price tag. You may find this somewhat frustrating and ask why can't your web designer just quote you a flat price? The reason for this is *project creep*. (And no, I am not calling your web designer a creep!) Your web designer realizes that your finished website will be bigger and more complex than you contemplated in your initial meeting. Typically what happens is that as the project gets underway, you become more aware of features or content you want in your website. As you add these features and content to your wish list, you are expanding the size, complexity, length of completion time, and development cost of the website. This is known as project (or scope) creep. Sometimes even what may seem to you like a minor change may have a ripple effect on the entire project, resulting in added cost and delay.

Also, when deciding on features that you want in your website, be realistic. Don't expect the Coca-Cola website on Bob's Sandwich Shoppe's budget!

By now you are probably asking "How long will it take to get my website up and running so that customers can visit it?" Of course, a lot will depend on how soon your designer can fit your project into his or her schedule. But once work on your project has begun, a standard informational website of seven-to-10 pages may be created within two-to-three weeks, assuming that you have provided your designer with all of the content planned for the site. More complex sites may take longer. The designer can also register your domain name, which usually takes four-to-five days, so that by the time the registration process is completed the designer is ready to start uploading your website to the server.

As he completes pages, your designer will probably upload the work-in-progress website to his server where it will be accessible only to you. You can then log on to the Internet and see your website as the designer works on it and inform him of changes that you would like to have made. Once you are satisfied with it, your designer will make the site accessible to everyone by transferring it to your chosen web host. That way you will know that you are satisfied with your website before it "goes live" and is visible by all. After all, you don't want a website on the Internet that everyone can access that you're not happy with!

Chapter Three

 The Web Designer's Client Handbook

CHAPTER FOUR

---

12 THINGS YOU NEVER THOUGHT OF (BUT SHOULD HAVE!)

1 - Cross-Browser Compatibility

NEITHER YOU NOR YOUR web designer knows what operating systems visitors to your website will be using. Some may use Microsoft Windows, some may use Apple Macintosh, while still others may use Linux, Unix, or FreeBSD. Additionally, there may be several versions of each operating system in use. Hyper Text Mark-up Language (HTML) enables web pages to be viewed across all operating systems.

A web browser is required to interpret HTML into a viewable format. Some of the more popular web browsers include Microsoft Internet Explorer, Firefox, Netscape, Opera, Mozilla, Safari (Apple), Konqueror (Linux), AOL (America On Line), Lynx (text only), and Simply Talker (for the blind). Even if two visitors are using the same browser, they may be using different versions of it. Ideally it is the goal of the web designer to ensure that your website will look the same no matter what browser the visitor is using.

The problem with goals is that they can not always be met. Of course, we still want to come as close as we can. The World Wide Web Consortium (W3C) sets HTML standards; the idea behind setting standards is that your web page should look the same regardless of which browser is used to access the page. If all of the web browser software companies followed W3C standards strictly then we could achieve our goal of uniformity. Unfortunately, the WC3 standards are voluntary, so most of the browser companies (with the exception of Opera) have added their own tweaks which may not work in competitors' browsers. The result is that a page designed to look one way in Internet Explorer may look totally different, or not even show up, in Netscape, Firefox, or Opera.

When designing your site, the designer must keep in mind that not everyone will be viewing your site with the same browser that you or your designer use. If you want everyone to be able to view your site properly, you must stick to WC3 standards — any deviation will reduce the number of people who can view your site properly.

2 - Cross-Platform Compatibility

Platforms refer to the operating system used. There are some differences in the way things will appear on a PC versus how they will appear on a Mac. Both fonts and colors vary by platform. When choosing a font for your website you must keep in mind that the font you choose may not be available on the visitor's computer. In that case, your designer must specify a default font (from that operating system's common fonts) or the visitor's operating system will automatically assign a default font of its own, with the result that the page — when viewed on that computer — may not look at all as you wished it to appear.

Font size is another casualty of the cross-platform wars. PCs display font type at 96 dpi (dots per inch), whereas Macs display font types at 72 dpi. The result is that fonts will look even smaller on a Mac than on a PC.

Another cross-platform difference is how colors are viewed. PC monitors are not as bright as Mac monitors, so the sharpness of the colors on your website will vary.

3 - User browser settings may override designer settings

Browsers are very configurable. The user can decide whether to turn off JavaScript, Active X, or even images. Users can also override website style sheets with their own, thus changing the font faces, font sizes, link colors, and other elements on a web page. The result is that elements on your page may look completely different from the way you intended them to look, or may not even load at all!

Users can also set the screen resolution on their monitors. "Screen resolution" refers to the number of individual pixels that fit within a given space. In an 800 x 600 resolution, 800 refers to number of pixels that monitor can display horizontally, while 600 refers to vertical limit. Resolution is a function of monitor size and user selection. A different screen size can dramatically change the way your page appears! If you have a graphic or a table that is 850 pixels wide and the viewer is using 800 x 600 resolution, he will have to scroll horizontally to see everything! Meanwhile, the visitor using a screen resolution of 1600 x 1200 may notice a large blank area on the right margin of his screen. A professional web designer will know how to compensate for differing screen resolutions.

4 - Blind visitors

At first it may seem like an oxymoron — blind website viewers? However, it is true that both blind and vision-impaired individuals regularly surf the web. Blind visitors use web browsers that read the text out loud. Text readers work fine until the browser reaches a picture or other graphic on your site. This is a case where one picture actually isn't worth a thousand words! Since it is a picture, the talking browser cannot "read" it, so your blind visitor is literally left in the dark wondering what the rest of the text was referring to. However, there is a way to let the blind visitors "read" your website's pictures. Your designer can include ALT attributes in the HTML; the speaking browser will read out loud whatever text appears in the ALT attributes. The ALT attribute is not visible in browsers unless the user places the mouse directly over the graphic. This can be useful where the user has purposely turned off his images in his browser settings (to improve download speed), is using a text-only browser, or where the image may be broken (due to a bad link or missing image file on the server) and not appear. With very large images, viewers can read the ALT attribute description as the image is loading.

Remember, your site should also be accessible to the visually-impaired. When planning your site with your web designer, avoid garish backgrounds that make text impossible to read and background colors that do not contrast well with the font colors. Also, keep in mind that many people suffer from red-green or yellow-blue color blindness.

5 - Font availability on the user's computer

No matter what font you choose to work with in designing the site on your computer, that font will only show up on the viewer's screen if he has that font on his computer; otherwise the viewer's operating system will default to an available font.

Chapter Four

The only way to guarantee that your chosen font will be seen is to save the text as a GIF (image) file (but this slows page loading; also some viewers may have image viewing turned off on their browsers).

Serifs (letters with feet) are more difficult to read in small scale and are best suited for body text. Sans Serifs (letters without feet) are best for very small (8 pt.) text or very large text (headlines). Font selection and use should be consistent throughout the site. Since PCs display font type at 96 dpi and Macs display at 72 dpi, fonts viewed on a PC will look even smaller to your viewers on a Mac.

6 - Color display may vary by monitor

Different monitors display colors differently. Different browsers also display colors differently. Some viewers, mostly males, are colorblind. Many people suffer from red-green or yellow-blue color blindness. So your colors may look different depending on the monitor used, the browser used, and the viewer.

Take care to avoid garish backgrounds that make text impossible to read while making the page look bad (paisley does not make a good background for text!).

7 - Color display on monitor (RGB) versus printer (CYMK)

After all the time you spent with your web designer selecting your color scheme, you are shocked and frustrated when the color printout of your website looks nothing like the colors on your screen. Why do colors look different on paper from the way they look on monitors? The reason is because paper and monitors view colors differently. The print medium uses subtractive colors, *i.e.,* colors that create black when mixed together (known as the CMYK color scheme). Computer monitors display additive colors, *i.e.,* colors that when mixed together create white (the RGB color scheme).

8 - Optimization of photos

Your website graphics should be aesthetically pleasing (*e.g.,* avoid two dozen animated GIFs on a page), relevant to the page content, and fast-loading (*i.e.,* small file size).

Website visitors are an impatient breed; they expect to see your web pages load immediately into their browsers. Every element on your web page — text, graphics, backgrounds — is actually a file stored on the server. The larger the file, the longer it (and ultimately the page) takes to load. Text files are quite small but graphics files can be immense. Remembering that viewers are impatient — they will not wait long for your graphics to appear — the goal is to reduce file size as much as possible. Your web designer can achieve this goal through the use of thumbnails, low source images, and photo optimization. Depending on the image involved and the techniques used, it is possible to reduce graphics file size by at least

50% without perceptibly affecting image quality. Savings of 90% or more are not uncommon. For example, the photo you took with your digital camera, after photo optimization, may be reduced to one-tenth of its original file size. If you have four or five such pictures on a page, imagine how much faster your page will load thanks to optimization!

Photo optimization is achieved using special graphics software. Your web designer must balance file size with image quality loss. He may also reduce file size by reducing the size of the image through cropping and image reduction.

9 - Browser Cache

As mentioned above, speed is the key on the web. Every time you reload a page in your browser, it contacts the server and begins to download each and every file that makes up your web page. Depending on the number and size of files, this process could take some time, so sometimes your browser cheats! The first time it loads a page the browser stores all of the files in a cache folder on your computer. Then, when it refreshes the page, instead of contacting the server it pulls the files from the cache on your own computer, which is much faster.

However, this caching can have some unintended consequences. Suppose a designer's client posts on its website photos of local children attending a client-sponsored charity event. Later, the client calls the designer and says that due to the complaint from a parent, a particular child must be cropped out of the photo immediately. The designer crops the photo and posts the replacement online right away. A week later the designer receives another call from an exasperated client wanting to know why the original picture is still on the website. The designer goes to the site and says "No, I'm looking at it right now, the cropped photo is there," and the client replies "No it isn't, I'm looking at it and I see the original photo." What happened? Who's right?

They both are. The cropped photo is on the website but the client's browser is pulling the photo from the cache on the client's computer, not from the server where the cropped photo is. The client needs to empty the cache and reload the page to see the cropped photo.

Learn where your browser keeps its History and Cache folders.

In Internet Explorer, go to TOOLS → INTERNET OPTIONS → TEMPORARY INTERNET FILES and delete the files.

In Firefox, go to TOOLS → OPTIONS → PRIVACY and clear the files.

In Opera, go to TOOLS → PREFERENCES → ADVANCED → HISTORY and empty the disk cache.

10 - Case sensitive servers

Some servers are case sensitive. That means if your file holding the picture of Sally is named "sally.jpg" and you have a link to "Sally. jpg" the server will not realize that Sally with a capital "S" and sally with a lower case "s" are supposed to refer to the same file. The browser will ask the server for Sally.jpg and the server will reply "Nope, no Sally.jpg here, just sally. jpg" and the result is that Sally's picture will not appear on your page. So capitalization (or lack thereof) in file names is very important if you are dealing with a case-sensitive server. If pages or graphics do not load properly or links do not work, a case-sensitive server is often the culprit.

11 - Backward compatible design (old browser versions still in use)

A legacy browser is an older version of an existing browser format. As an older version, the legacy browser may not be able to accommodate certain features, such as frames, or it may ship without many of today's standard plug-ins, like Macromedia Flash. As you work with your designer to construct your website you must balance your desire for cutting edge technology with the realization that many potential visitors to your site are still using legacy browsers that may not be able to accommodate the latest technology.

12 - Forward compatible design

Conversely, you and your designer will also want to be continually adapting to new technologies, such as DHTML, CSS, and Flash. New technologies, especially multi-media, can enhance a website when used appropriately, but you must exercise caution and restraint. Some visitors find it annoying for music to start playing automatically. They may not have the volume set properly on their speakers, or they may be listening to something else. Viewers in an office setting (or their bosses) might not appreciate an unexpected loud sound coming from their computer!

Audio may enhance your website but remember that you don't know what your visitor's computer looks like. Obviously he or she needs speakers to hear your audio. The playback quality depends on the process and format used to make the audio file as well as the quality of the visitor's speakers and sound card.

Finally, if you choose to incorporate multi-media into your website, make sure that any audio or video you use on your site is owned by you or is in public domain; do not put copyrighted songs or videos on your site!

CHAPTER FIVE

LEGAL ISSUES

As a website owner, you may be legally responsible for certain aspects of your website. While this is a very important area, we will not cover it in depth because there is so much to cover one could write an entire book devoted to the subject. In fact, we have another book, also available from Amber Book Company, called *Issues In Internet Law* that does go into much greater detail. (Available from www.AmberBookCompany.com or www.IssuesInInternetLaw.com). What we will do in this chapter is try to highlight key areas with which you should be concerned.

Copyright

You will automatically have a common law copyright on anything you create and place on your website. You may, if you wish, register your copyright with the U.S. Copyright Office. You should display your copyright information on your website like this: "Entire site contents © 2006 My Website, Inc. All Rights Reserved." Use the © symbol, not (c). You can also specify specific content (text or graphics) as copyrighted.

Be sure that any content you use on your site is owned by you, used with written permission, or in the public domain. "Public domain" does not mean that the content was freely available to the public, such as on another website. Public domain means that the copyright protection has expired or was never available to the content in the first place.

Do not put copyrighted graphics on your site! Examples of copyrighted material include photos or graphics you found on another website, songs you want to add to your site, and articles from other sources. If a newspaper wrote a glowing review of your business, even though the whole article is about you, it is copyrighted by the newspaper and can not be used on your website without the newspaper's permission. Even if you licensed material for use in your promotional materials (say a licensed photo for your company brochure) unless it is a broad license you would be violating the licensor's copyright by reusing it on your website.

And of course, if you shouldn't put copyrighted work on your site, neither should anyone else!

Legal Issues

If you have sections of your site where you allow visitors to upload or contribute material, then you must constantly be vigilant against the possibility that they may place copyrighted work on your site. Did they upload a copyrighted photo or cut and paste a copyrighted article onto your site? Remember, simply placing the other party's copyright information below the item does not give you permission to post it on your site.

One final word about copyright — under U.S. law, the creator of the work is deemed to be the copyright holder, so the creator of your website actually holds the copyright to it. By default, the web designer becomes the copyright owner unless the contract states otherwise. Most web designers, in their contracts, will either assign the copyright to the client (while retaining a license to use the work in their portfolio) or grant the client a license to use the work on the site.

Trademark

Trademark issues usually arise when you select your domain name. Generally, you do not want to choose a domain name that incorporates part or all of a trademarked name. Doing so might subject you to liability under the Anti-Cybersquatting Consumer Protection Act if the court finds you deliberately and in bad faith registered a domain name in violation of the rights of the trademark owner. But it may not be so clear cut. Suppose three businesses wish to register "apple.com." One is a major wholesaler of apples, one is a music record label, and one is a computer manufacturer. Obviously there is no bad faith motive behind any of the three firms — each has a legitimate business reason to register the domain name. Each firm may have trademarked the name within its home state, and one may even have a federal trademark. But having a trademark alone does not automatically guarantee the right to a domain name; the trademark owner must show both that the domain name registrant had a "bad faith intent to profit from" a trademark and that the registrant registered, trafficked in, or used a domain name identically or confusingly similar to the trademark.

Defamation

Defamation is a "published intentional false communication that injures a person or company's reputation." Defamation can be written (libel) or spoken (slander). If the statement is true, then it is not defamation (truth is a legal defense to a charge of defamation). As a website owner, you want to make sure that nothing on your site, whether posted by you or anyone else, is defamatory. Watch what you say about other individuals or competitors — if you don't think you could back up your words with proof in a court of law, don't say it!

Blogs and message boards can be especially hazardous, because comments in them are often written and posted in the heat of the moment without prolonged thought or review.

Your "shoot from the hip" reply may get you in trouble, so always review your posts with consideration for defamation in mind.

And as with copyright, you must be alert for what others may post or say on your website. It is probably not a good idea to let your more enthusiastic customers post on your website how one of your particular competitors is "a crook who deals in stolen merchandise."

Something else you probably do not want on your website is pornography. Unless you are running a sex site, it is probably a good idea to review what you (or others) allow on your site. Obscenity laws vary by state and by country and the notion of what is or is not "obscene" has been a murky issue long before the Internet sprang into existence.

While it is O.K. to send e-mail to your friends and customers, sending mass amounts of unsolicited e-mail is considered spam. Nobody likes spam. You will not gain new friends and improve your reputation by spamming. While sending spam is not illegal, it is frowned on by everyone from ISPs and hosting companies to the ultimate recipients. In fact, your ISP or hosting company may bar you if you do spam. While the CAN-SPAM Act of 2003 does not ban sending spam, it requires the use of accurate headers in e-mail messages and procedures for recipients to opt out of future e-mails, and forbids e-mail address harvesting. Spam that does not comply with the Act may be illegal. There are other circumstances when spam may be illegal. Trademark and unfair competition laws have been used against spammers who identify their messages as coming from someone else. Spam containing misleading or false statements can trigger Federal Trade Commission review under the Truth in Advertising laws.

It is certainly permissible to use e-mail as a marketing tool. E-mail can be a very cost-effective marketing tool. The best approach is to use permission-based marketing, by allowing visitors to your website to sign up to receive your e-mails. If they have "opted-in" to be on your list, then anything you send them is not spam.

Marketing and COPPA Requirements

If you are targeting children with your website or if you believe your site will attract a large number of young visitors, then you need to be aware of COPPA and its requirements.

The Children's Online Privacy Protection Act (COPPA) controls how websites can collect and/or maintain personal information about children. The Act defines a "child" as under age 13. COPPA applies to "websites directed at children" or where the "site knows it is collecting information from children."

COPPA requires that the website:

- Provide parents with notice of the website's information practices
- Obtain prior verifiable parental consent before collecting information from a child
- Provide the parent, upon request, with the right to view information submitted by the child
- Provide the parent with the opportunity to prevent further use or collection of information
- Limit the collection of information required to participate in games or prize offers, and
- Provide reasonable procedures to protect the confidentiality, security, and integrity of personal information it receives

Under COPPA, the website must provide notice about its information collection practices. The notice must be posted from a link on the home page and on each page where information is collected from children. The website must obtain verifiable parental consent *before* collecting, using, or disclosing any information from a child. Some websites have given up collecting information collection from children, citing the process of compliance with COPPA as too burdensome. However, the website does not need verifiable parental consent if it is responding directly on one-time basis to a child and the information is not retained, or if it is reasonably necessary to protect safety of child or to protect the security and integrity of the website.

Chapter Five

For More In-depth Coverage

The Internet is a new technology that presents many novel legal issues. As a website owner or website designer you should be aware of all of these issues and stay current on changes in the law. We recommend those interested read ***Issues In Internet Law*** (ISBN #0977161102), available from Amazon.com or AmberBookCompany.com.

CHAPTER SIX

ALL ABOUT E-MAIL

Your E-Mail Address

WITH YOUR DOMAIN NAME, you get potentially unlimited e-mail addresses. You can choose any name to put in front of your domain name such as bob@yourcompany.com, sales@yourcompany.com, orders@yourcompany.com, and it all goes into your domain's mail box in your server space. You can check your e-mail from any computer with Internet access using an e-mail program. You can get your mail no matter where you are as long as you have access to the Internet.

You may already have a personal e-mail account with a service like AOL, Hotmail, Yahoo, or Gmail. However, it is far more professional to have an e-mail address that includes your business name. "You@YourBusiness.com" not only promotes your business through branding, but sounds much more professional to your customers than "sexykitten@hotmail.com."

There are two ways to retrieve e-mail: web-based and through an e-mail client. Your e-mail is sent to a mail server (think of this as a post office). The name of the server usually follows the "@" symbol in your e-mail address. You can either read your e-mail on the server or download it from the server to your computer.

Web-Based E-Mail

To read it on the server, you go to the server's mail website (*e.g.*, Hotmail, Yahoo Mail, or *yourwebsite.com*). In many cases, you can access your web-based e-mail from your own site by typing http://domain.com/webmail/ where domain.com is your domain name and the login username is your e-mail address. Web-based e-mail is like going to the post-office, reading your mail there, and going home. And if you have more than one e-mail address, you have to go to more than one web page. That's like going to several post offices, standing there reading your mail, and going home; it's not very efficient.

E-Mail Clients

To download your e-mail from the server, you need to use an e-mail client (*i.e.*, software). The most-used client is Microsoft Outlook and/or Outlook Express;

not necessarily because it is the best client, but because Outlook Express comes as part of every Microsoft Windows operating system and Outlook is part of the Microsoft Office Suite used by most businesses. Because Outlook is used on almost all Windows computers, and because most viruses are transmitted through e-mail, almost all e-mail viruses target specific known weaknesses in Outlook. For this and many other reasons, you may wish to use an alternative e-mail client. For a list of all e-mail clients, type "e-mail clients" into download.com or google.com.

One highly customizable alternative e-mail client is The Bat!, available from www.ritlabs.com/en/products/thebat/. The trial version is free; full versions start at $25. The Bat! is a powerful, highly configurable, yet easy to use e-mail client. It protects your computer from viruses and worms that spread by e-mail and does not use the Windows address book and Windows-dependent HTML viewer, which have been the targets of many recent virus attacks. It warns the user before opening suspicious attachments or even blocks them completely. The Bat! supports unlimited number of accounts and users; you can receive mail from multiple e-mail addresses (home, business, personal, website, etc.) all in one session. It has fully customizable message templates that save hours of typing, and you can add signature files to your e-mails. The scheduler notifies about upcoming events, birthdays, postponed messages and performs other automated tasks. You can color code messages and put photos and contact info in its address book. It also has a multi-lingual interface supporting 15 languages.

Besides The Bat!, popular e-mail clients include Eudora, Pegasus, and Mozilla Thunderbird.

In addition to an e-mail client, you may wish to use a buffer between the mail server and your computer to filter out spam. Mailwasher Pro (www.mailwasher.net) is an example of anti-spam software that allows you to delete spam, viruses, and other unwanted e-mails right at the server before they can be downloaded to your computer.

Mailing Lists

Besides e-mail, you may also create multiple mailing lists. Each list may contain an unlimited number of e-mail addresses. With a single mouse-click you will be able to e-mail every name on the list. You can set up multiple mailing lists, *e.g.,* one for customers, one for suppliers, and one for people who choose to opt-in to your newsletter. However, be sure not to use your mailing lists to spam others!

CHAPTER SEVEN

PROMOTION & SEARCH ENGINE OPTIMIZATION

The internet is very large with millions of websites. "How is anyone going to find my website?," you may ask. Promotion and search engine optimization are the keys to attracting traffic to your website.

Promotion

You can promote your website both offline and online. Offline methods of promotion include printing your URL (website address) on business cards, letterhead, and brochures, as well as in print and television ads and on mailers (flyers and postcards). You can also write articles for various publications and include your URL with your biographical information.

Online, you can promote your site by including your website's URL in the text signature line at the bottom of your e-mails. You can also include your URL in your signature line whenever you post to Usenet news groups. You can find various news groups by searching on Google Groups (http://groups.google.com). However, make sure that your posts appear related to the topics and do not come across as spam or you may anger the very people you are trying to attract.

Another method of online promotion is through the use of hypertext links. Find a trade or industry website and see if they will agree to place a link to your website on their site. Seek out reciprocal links by offering to place a link to someone's site on your website if they will link to yours. Have your designer create some banner ads and provide instructions on your site for others to download your banners and place them on their sites. There are even banner exchange sites where you can exchange reciprocal banner ads with other website owners.

On your website itself, you can ask visitors to bookmark your site, so they will be more likely to return. You can offer them the option of signing up for your mailing list or to receive your e-mailed newsletter. Supply your designer with a list of key words to place in your website's meta tags to steer search engines toward your site. Also ask your designer to use key words in the title of each page on your site (search engines often search the HTML "Title" tag on a web page). And of course, you or your web designer should submit your completed website to search engines and directories.

Finally, you can pay to promote your website. E-mail lists can be rented and used to send out announcements. Some websites sell advertising space. And search engines offer "pay per click" advertising. With pay per click, you select key words which, when entered into the search engine, pull up a link to your website; you then are charged each time the link is clicked on by a searcher. The more you are willing to pay per click, the higher your site will appear in the results for your chosen keywords.

Search Engine Optimization

As you can see from the preceding section, search engines play a large role in driving traffic to your website. The higher your search engine ranking, the more likely you are to turn searchers into visitors to your website.

Search engines list your site in one of two ways: submission of your site information, or through spiders and robots that crawl the web. Once the search engine has your information, it will either automatically add your listing or hold your listing pending review by a human (which may take anywhere from 6-to-24 months, based on their backlog of sites to be reviewed).

Chapter Seven

Your website's placement (ranking) in a given search engine is based on:
  (1) meta tags used in the HTML of your web pages
  (2) key words used on the web page
  (3) a formula used by the search engine, and
  (4) payment

There are hundreds of search engines, but only a dozen or so "biggies." Each search engine uses its own formula for placement. For example, Google may place you higher if you have 12 or more keywords in your meta tags, while Lycos may penalize you if you have more than nine words. So the placement criteria may be mutually exclusive for different search engines. And even more frustratingly, search engines routinely and periodically change their formulas and criteria to make sure no one can "beat" the system. What works today to generate a higher placement for you may not work tomorrow! Search engine optimization is the methodology of making your website accessible to search engines to ensure that your pages will be ranked highly. Nevertheless, you may do everything right and still have 20 pages of listings ahead of you. Why? Because search engines allow anyone who pays them a placement fee to cut to the front of the line!!

What is the best way to guarantee high placement? Unfortunately, either by paying a placement fee to each engine you are concerned about, and/or by hiring a search engine placement firm to keep you abreast of each search engine's ever-changing criteria.

For an excellent overview of search engines, visit SearchEngineWatch.com (http:// searchenginewatch.com/webmasters/index.php).

CHAPTER EIGHT

WEB DESIGN CONTRACTS

There are three types of contracts that your web designer may present to you. The web design contract contains the agreements between you and your designer pertaining to construction of your website. The web maintenance contract provides for routine work done on your site after completion of the construction of the site. The web hosting contract is the agreement between you and your hosting company (which may or may not be your designer).

Boiler Plate

Like all contracts, there are certain boiler-plate provisions common to all three. The contract may begin with a definition of terms used in the document. While at first glance it may seem unnecessary to define everyday phrases, a lot of misunderstandings and problems can be avoided by spelling out what is meant by key phrases. For example, suppose the contract states something is to occur within 10 days. Is that 10 calendar days or 10 business days? On Friday the 1st, the 10th calendar day would be Monday the 11th; however, the 10th business day would be Friday the 15th! Depending on how "day" is understood by the parties, the deadline could be the first day of the week or the last day of the week!

The contract should also designate an authorized individual to act as the liaison between the client and the designer. Many problems can arise when the designer is given conflicting instructions from multiple parties working for the client. Choose one person to be given the authority to serve as the contact person in your organization for your dealings with your designer.

Most contracts will contain an authorization clause for the client to allow the designer to access the client's server, either to upload the final website or to provide regular site maintenance.

There will be a clause relating to the payment of fees — how often payments are to be made, in what amounts, and by what payment methods. There may also be a provision for reimbursement of the designer's expenses, such as telephone charges, postage, shipping, courier charges, travel expenses, and fees paid to subcontractors. There will likely be penalties for late payment described as well.

Web Design Contracts

The contract will contain limitations of liability such as that operation of the web pages is not guaranteed to be uninterrupted or error-free. It will also state that the designer will not be liable for claims by third parties (such as defamation or intellectual property claims) based on the content provided by the client and will be indemnified against such claims by the client. It will also spell out that the client represents that he has authority to enter into the contract and that none of the content (*e.g.*, text, graphics, photos, designs, and trademarks) provided to the designer is copyrighted material or that he has written permission to use such materials.

There will often be a clause allowing the designer (or hosting company) to use subcontractors on your project.

The liquidated damages clause states what your financial responsibility will be if you breach the contract. Other boiler-plate clauses establish the venue (location) for any potential lawsuits or arbitration claims under the contract, the fact that the contract is the only binding agreement between you and your designer (agreements over coffee or phone calls don't count—only what is contained within the contract), and a statement that if any clause in the contract is declared invalid by a court, the rest of the contract will remain enforceable.

Chapter Eight

The Web Design Contract

The web design contract is an agreement between you and your web designer regarding the terms and conditions related to the project of building your website. It also spells out the rights and responsibilities of both you and your web designer. The contract remains in force only until completion of the project. It should specify a completion date and provisions should the client decides he needs a "rush job."

The contract should describe the nature of the project, *i.e.*, whether it is a standard website package offered by the designer, a custom job, or an e-commerce application. It may provide that after completion of the project you may have the option to purchase an on-going maintenance program from the designer.

One of the biggest problems a web designer faces in quoting a client a price on the project is that clients often fail to provide the website content to the designer in a timely manner or they make significant changes midway through the project. The contract may attempt to compensate for this by making prices quoted in the contract conditional upon performance by the client. The contract may provide that you have a responsibility to cooperate with your designer, provide him with all of the necessary website content at the outset, not make changes or revisions to previously submitted material, and not cause any delays in the project. Remember, your designer quoted you a price based on the amount of time and effort your project required according to your initial representations at the outset; changes in the size or scope of the project will most likely be accompanied by a corresponding change in the cost. Also, your designer has budgeted his time to work on your project; any delays you cause may force him to take time away from someone else's project! For these reasons, the contract may provide a framework to accommodate changes in project scope.

So make sure you supply your web designer with all of the text, graphics, designs, written permissions to use copyrighted materials, and color schemes before work actually begins on the project. If you schedule meetings with your designer, show up! Only give your designer your final text drafts; designers hate wasting time revising the same client-submitted text after a web page has been constructed.

The contract should provide that you own the copyright or have written permission to use any text, graphics, photos, designs, trademarks, or other artwork furnished to your designer for inclusion on your website. There should also be a provision describing which rights your designer is assigning to you and which rights he is retaining. Such a clause may read as follows:

Upon final payment under the terms of this Agreement, Client is assigned rights to use as a website the design, graphics, and text contained in the finished assembled website. Rights to photos, graphics, source code, work-up files, and computer programs are specifically not transferred to Client, and remain the

property of their respective owners. Designer and its agents retain the right to display graphics and other web design elements as examples of their work in their respective portfolios. Designer grants Client a nonexclusive, nontransferable, royalty-free license to use said Developer Content. This license shall authorize Client to: operate the site on its host server; update, revise, or republish the site; and advertise and promote the site. Client agrees that the inclusion of a copyright notice on the site in the name of the client, (*e.g.,* ©2006 Client) does not affect any of the rights or provisions of this paragraph, and that said notice applies only to Client Content and not to Developer Content, and that any actual copyright and/or license is not assigned to Client until final payment has been made by Client to Designer.

The contract may include charges for hosting the site on the designer's server if you delay in arranging permanent hosting. And finally, the web design contract may have a clause allowing the designer to state on your website that he created the site and/or link to the designer's home page and link from the designer's site back to your website (as an example of his web design work).

Web Maintenance Contract

The web maintenance contract is very similar to the web design contract except that its focus is on the on-going maintenance of the website after the initial development project has been completed. The contract is typically a one year renewable agreement, unlike the web design contract which lasts only until completion of the project.

Web Design Contracts

Usually the maintenance contract includes minor web page maintenance to regular web pages (*e.g.,* updating links and making minor changes to a sentence or paragraph). Most designers will exclude major revisions (*e.g.,* removing nearly all the text from a page and replacing it with new text) from their maintenance programs).

There may be a provision that if you let someone else work on your website and they mess it up fixing it will not fall under the maintenance contract. The contract may specify what work is not considered "maintenance" and what additional charges may apply for such work.

Web Hosting Contract

The web hosting contract should describe the terms and features of the specific hosting package you have chosen. Most web hosts offer multiple packages with varying degrees of features and services. Variable features will include the amount of hard drive space, the amount of allowable monthly data transfer, the number of sub-domains, FTP accounts, MySQL Databases, POP3 accounts, and mailing lists. If there is an initial setup fee that should be disclosed in the contract as well. The contract will also state the maximum allowable monthly bandwidth (traffic caused by visitors to your site) and any surcharges if the monthly bandwidth amount is exceeded.

Chapter Eight

    The Web Designer's Client Handbook

CHAPTER NINE

TROUBLE-SHOOTING

Help! My website is down!

THE DREADED WORDS YOU never want to hear spill from your lips! Brace yourself! All websites experience some downtime. Your site may be down briefly for routine scheduled maintenance on the server or it may be temporarily inaccessible due to heavy Internet traffic.

Sometimes, of course, there may be other reasons your website is down. It may be inaccessible because of problems with your Internet Service Provider (ISP) or due to a network problem between your computer and your website server. This may occur for several reasons—the Internet connection went down, the ISP is having network problems or your web server has failed.

There may be times when instead of reaching your website you are greeted by an error message. Often the error message will hold the key to the problem.

"The server does not have a DNS entry," indicates that the URL you entered into your browser's address bar had an error—either yours or your referring source's. Recheck the URL and make sure that you capitalized the letters that should be capitalized (remember from Chapter Four that some servers are case-sensitive) and spelled everything correctly. However, if you repeatedly get DNS errors, contact your (ISP) and ask them to update their locally cached DNS files.

"The website and/or server you are trying to access is busy." Sometimes the server is swamped with too many requests. Try accessing the website again; you can often reach it on the second or third try.

"Error 404 – File Not Found." We have all seen this error message at some point in our web surfing. Besides making you wonder what the first 403 error messages are, the Error 404 – File Not Found error tells you that the server was unable to find the file or program corresponding to the document that you requested. This may happen for several reasons, including a typographical error on your part (if the URL was misspelled then the server will be looking for a file name that doesn't exist) or a missing file—it's possible that the file was removed, renamed, or is otherwise unavailable. (With a case-sensitive server, if a file is replaced with a change in capitalization of the file name, the server will not recognize requests for the original name).

Trouble-Shooting

"Host unavailable." This error usually occurs when the host server is down. You can try to access the site again by clicking the "Reload" button on your browser.

"Network connection was refused by the server or too many connections." This error occurs when the server is too busy to handle more traffic. You can try the site again by clicking your browser's "Reload" button or try again later.

If you cannot access your website but are not receiving one of the error messages above, there may be something preventing your computer from reaching the site. You may have one or more firewalls on your computer that is blocking your access. Sometimes newly installed software can change existing firewall settings. If you use a router to connect to the Internet, remember that routers also have built-in firewalls. Your ISP may also have a firewall set to block certain content or IP addresses. Try contacting your ISP if you have determined that you do not have a firewall blocking the site. Likewise, your hosting company may blacklist certain ISPs that they have identified as major sources of spam. If you have disabled all of the firewalls on your end, cleared your browser cache, and verified your hosts file, then it is likely that either your ISP is blocking your website's IP address or your host server is blocking your ISP's address.

INDEX

A

B

C

D

Index

Index

screen resolution 28
search engine 11, 21, 49, 51, 52
search engine optimization 49, 51, 52
spam 41, 42, 48, 50, 63
static website 4, 16
style 16, 20, 28

T

template designer 9
Three Click Rule 15
trademark 39, 42

U

URL 49, 50, 62

W

web-based e-mail 46
web browser 25, 26
web design contract 53, 56, 58
web hosting contract 53, 59
web maintenance contract 53, 58
World Wide Web iii, 11, 14, 26

Printed in the United States
77553LV00004B/12